AF316748

Horses

This is us

Susana Conde

Equibooks
equibooks@yahoo.com

First Edition 2019

ISBN: 978-84-949876-0-1

Horses are prey
animals

To be safe,
they live in herds

They are always on the alert in order to detect any possible threats in good time

When they are scared,
their heads get high,
their necks and
mouths get tight,
they stop blinking
and they are unable
to eat

Check this horse
out, he is scared,
he doesn't express
it with words,
but with his body
language

When they feel in danger, they gallop off and flee as quickly as possible

Silently, and using only body language, they make
a joint, rapid decision with other herd members in
which direction to flee

The baby foals
can stand and
run with the
adults, just hours
after being born

And after all the
tension, when
they calm down
again, they lick
and chew, shake
their heads,
snort or yawn

That's why
they live in
open areas:
danger is more
difficult to
detect and
flee from
in enclosed
spaces

Their eyes are positioned at the
sides of their head, which enables
them to spot danger from whatever
direction it may come from

They have a
keen sense
of smell and
they use it to
investigate
everything
around them

And thanks
to those tiny
whiskers, they
can also do this
in darkness too

Their sight is
very sensitive
to movement

They have a
great sense of
hearing, and
if you look at
their ears you'll
know where
their attention
is focused

To run fast, they
have hooves
instead of toes

Their teeth grow
continually to
counteract the wear
caused by their diet

They don't fear the rain, their
coat protects them from the
cold and damp

They use their tails, or those of others, to shoo the flies away

When they feel
safe, they are
really curious
creatures

They have
close friends

They meet others with their nose, to
smell each other and get to know them

They use body language for communication

They scratch
one another

And in this way show their
affection

The little ones learn from
their elders

Keep moving is very important
and they travel long distances
every day

They love rolling on the dirt, especially when wet in order to dry themselves. But they also do this to stretch their muscles and just for fun

They spend most of the day grazing, eating little but
often so they don't get too full and heavy, which would
hinder them from running away at any time

They can sleep standing, but to rest
they need to lie flat, even though
they only sleep a few hours

Even then they remain vigilant, as they might be taken by surprise at any time

Paperback edition ISBN: 978-1798205310

Original title: Caballos ¿Quieres conocernos?
Hardback ISBN: 978-84-949876-2-5
Paperback ISBN: 978-1796306026

Revised by Julie Mills

Pictures 1,12 Christel. 3, 22 por B. Iyata. 4,30 J. D. Mers. 5 ,6, 7, 8, 11, 14, 16, 17, 20, 21, 26, 28, 31, 32 C. P Rolls
10 B. Brandon. 13 C. Candice. 15 I. Castro. 18 Alexandra. 19 A. Tångvik. 23 S. Stars. 24 D. Kudyba. 25 Wellox.
29 M. Langthim. 34 M. Muñoz

Typeface/Font created by Abelardo González designed to help with some symptoms of Dyslexia.

www.ingramcontent.com/pod-product-compliance
Lightning Source LLC
Chambersburg PA
CBHW042356140726
48196CB00017B/723